Home is where the

OCTOPUSSY

AGNEATHA

MOTLEY

SPIRO

AMON-RA

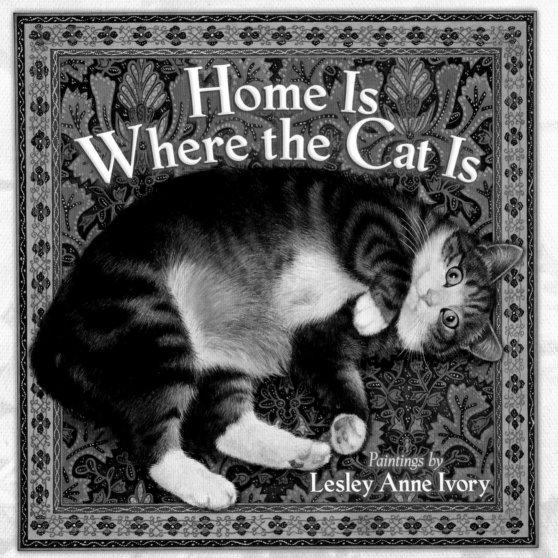

Home Is Where the Cat Is

Paintings by
Lesley Anne Ivory

HARVEST HOUSE PUBLISHERS

EUGENE, OREGON

HOME IS WHERE THE CAT IS

Text copyright © 2007 by Harvest House Publishers
Published by Harvest House Publishers
Eugene, Oregon 97402

ISBN-13: 978-0-7369-1848-0

Design and production by Garborg Design Works, Savage, Minnesota

Harvest House Publishers has made every effort to trace the ownership of all poems and quotes. In the event of a question arising from the use of a poem or quote, we regret any error made and will be pleased to make the necessary correction in future editions of this book.

Printed in China

08 09 10 11 12 13 / LP / 10 9 8 7 6 5 4 3 2

I love cats because
I enjoy my home;
and little by little,
they become its
visible soul.

JEAN COCTEAU

3

Like a graceful vase, a cat, even when motionless, seems to flow.

GEORGE F. WILL

The most domestic cat, which has lain on a rug all her days, appears quite at home in the woods, and, by her sly and stealthy behavior, proves herself more native there than the regular inhabitants.

HENRY DAVID THOREAU

Of all God's creatures there is only one that cannot be made the slave of the lash. That one is the cat. If man could be crossed with a cat it would improve man, but it would deteriorate the cat.

MARK TWAIN

You can keep a
dog; but it is the
cat who keeps
people, because
cats find humans
useful domestic
animals.

GEORGE MIKES

6

A cat sees no good reason why
it should obey another animal,
even if it does stand on two legs.

SARAH THOMPSON

I married early, and was happy to find in my wife a disposition not uncongenial with my own. Observing my partiality for domestic pets, she lost no opportunity of procuring those of the most agreeable kind. We had birds, goldfish, a fine dog, rabbits, a small monkey, and a cat.

This latter was a remarkably large and beautiful animal, entirely black, and sagacious to an astonishing degree....Pluto—this was the cat's name—was my favorite pet and playmate. I alone fed him, and he attended me wherever I went about the house. It was even with difficulty that I could prevent him from following me through the streets.

EDGAR ALLAN POE
The Black Cat

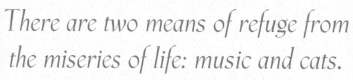

There are two means of refuge from
the miseries of life: music and cats.

ALBERT SCHWEITZER

The Marquis, making several low bows, accepted the honor which his Majesty conferred upon him, and forthwith, that very same day, married the Princess.

Puss became a great lord, and never ran after mice any more but only for his diversion.

ANDREW LANG
Puss in Boots

*Prowling his own quiet backyard
or asleep by the fire, he is still only
a whisker away from the wilds.*

JEAN BURDEN

Once upon a time there lived a queen who had a beautiful cat, the colour of smoke, with china-blue eyes, which she was very fond of. The cat was constantly with her, and ran after her wherever she went, and even sat up proudly by her side when she drove out in her fine glass coach.

"Oh, pussy," said the queen one day, "you are happier than I am! For you have a dear kitten just like yourself, and I have nobody to play with but you."

"Don't cry," answered the cat, laying her paw on her mistress's arm. "Crying never does any good. I will see what can be done."

The cat was as good as her word. As soon as she returned from her drive she trotted off to the forest to consult a fairy who dwelt there, and very soon after the queen had a little girl, who seemed made out of snow and sunbeams. The queen was delighted, and soon the baby began to take notice of the kitten as she jumped about the room, and would not go to sleep at all unless the kitten lay curled up beside her.

ANDREW LANG
Kisa the Cat

The smallest feline is a masterpiece.

LEONARDO DA VINCI

Since each of us is
blessed with only one life,
why not live it with a cat?

ROBERT STEARNS

A cat pours his body on
the floor like water. It is
restful just to see him.

WILLIAM LYON PHELPS

Of all domestic animals the cat is the most expressive. His face is capable of showing a wide range of expressions. His tail is a mirror of his mind. His gracefulness is surpassed only by his agility. And, along with all these, he has a sense of humor.

WALTER CHANDOHA

Nice pussy! Come and let me rub you!" said Freddie softly, as he held out his hand toward the stray cat.

"Yes, come here, Snoop!" added Flossie, as she walked along with her brother.

"'Tisn't Snoop, and you mustn't call him that name," ordered Freddie.

"Well, he looks like Snoop," declared Flossie.

"But if that isn't his name he won't like to be called by it, no more than if I called you Susie when your name's Flossie," went on the little boy.

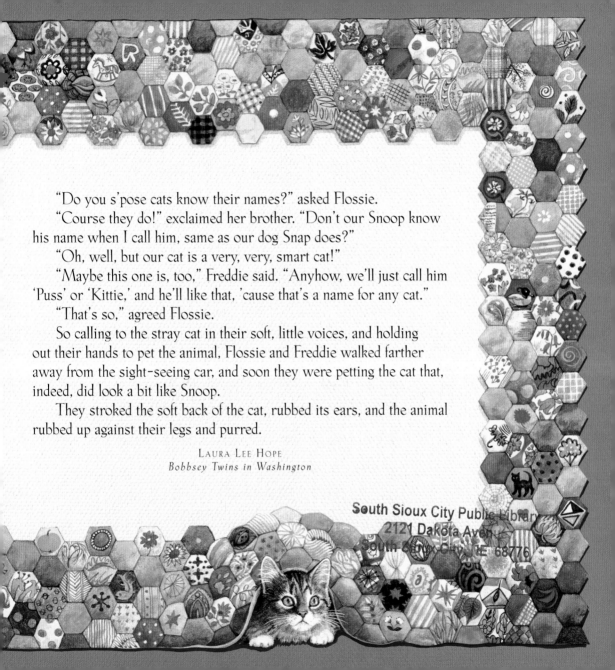

"Do you s'pose cats know their names?" asked Flossie.

"Course they do!" exclaimed her brother. "Don't our Snoop know his name when I call him, same as our dog Snap does?"

"Oh, well, but our cat is a very, very, smart cat!"

"Maybe this one is, too," Freddie said. "Anyhow, we'll just call him 'Puss' or 'Kittie,' and he'll like that, 'cause that's a name for any cat."

"That's so," agreed Flossie.

So calling to the stray cat in their soft, little voices, and holding out their hands to pet the animal, Flossie and Freddie walked farther away from the sight-seeing car, and soon they were petting the cat that, indeed, did look a bit like Snoop.

They stroked the soft back of the cat, rubbed its ears, and the animal rubbed up against their legs and purred.

LAURA LEE HOPE
Bobbsey Twins in Washington

Her function is to sit and be admired.

GEORGINA STRICKLAND GATES

A cat has absolute
emotional honesty:
human beings, for
one reason or
another, may hide
their feelings, but a
cat does not.

ERNEST HEMINGWAY

I don't suppose a more thoroughly contented personality is
to be found in all Chelsea," observed Jocantha in allusion to
herself; "except perhaps Attab," she continued, glancing towards
the large tabby-marked cat that lay in considerable ease in a
corner of the divan. "He lies there, purring and dreaming, shifting
his limbs now and then in an ecstasy of cushioned comfort. He
seems the incarnation of everything soft and silky and velvety,
without a sharp edge in his composition, a dreamer whose
philosophy is sleep and let sleep; and then, as evening draws on,
he goes out into the garden with a red glint in his eyes...."

H.H. MUNRO
The Philanthropist and the Happy Cat

*Cats are a mysterious
kind of folk. There is more
passing in their minds
than we are aware of.*

Sir Walter Scott

This cat was, for a cat,
needlessly tall, powerful,
independent and masculine.
Once, long ago, he had been
a roly-poly pepper-and-salt
kitten; he had a home in those
days, and a name, "Gipsy,"
which he abundantly justified.

Booth Tarkington
Penrod and Sam

If the pull of the outside world is strong, there is also a pull towards the human. The cat may disappear on its own errands, but sooner or later, it returns once again for a little while, to greet us with its own type of love. Independent as they are, cats find more than pleasure in our company.

LLOYD ALEXANDER

Hey, my kitten, my kitten,

Hey, my kitten, my deary;

Such a sweet pet as this

Was neither far nor neary.

CHILDREN'S NURSERY RHYME

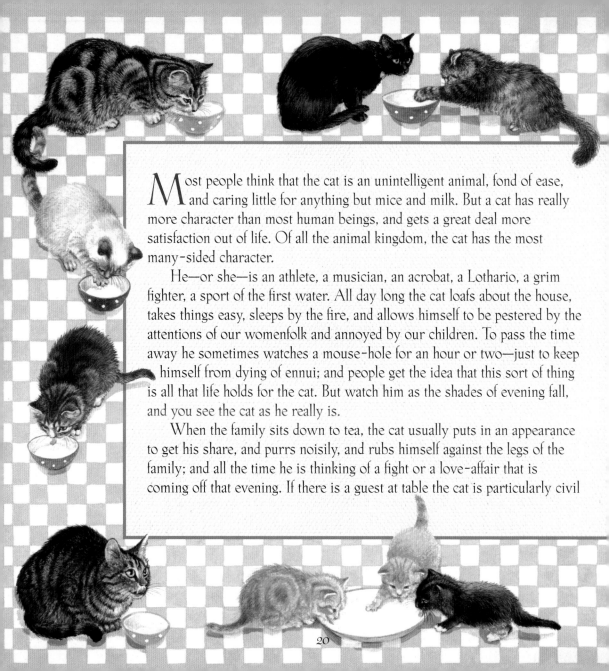

M ost people think that the cat is an unintelligent animal, fond of ease, and caring little for anything but mice and milk. But a cat has really more character than most human beings, and gets a great deal more satisfaction out of life. Of all the animal kingdom, the cat has the most many-sided character.

He—or she—is an athlete, a musician, an acrobat, a Lothario, a grim fighter, a sport of the first water. All day long the cat loafs about the house, takes things easy, sleeps by the fire, and allows himself to be pestered by the attentions of our womenfolk and annoyed by our children. To pass the time away he sometimes watches a mouse-hole for an hour or two—just to keep himself from dying of ennui; and people get the idea that this sort of thing is all that life holds for the cat. But watch him as the shades of evening fall, and you see the cat as he really is.

When the family sits down to tea, the cat usually puts in an appearance to get his share, and purrs noisily, and rubs himself against the legs of the family; and all the time he is thinking of a fight or a love-affair that is coming off that evening. If there is a guest at table the cat is particularly civil

to him, because the guest is likely to have the best of what is going. Sometimes, instead of recognizing this civility with something to eat, the guest stoops down and strokes the cat, and says, "Poor pussy! Poor pussy!"

The cat soon tires of that; he puts up his claw and quietly but firmly rakes the guest in the leg.

"Ow!" says the guest, "the cat stuck his claws into me!" The delighted family remarks, "Isn't it sweet of him? Isn't he intelligent? HE WANTS YOU TO GIVE HIM SOMETHING TO EAT."

The guest dares not do what he would like to do—kick the cat through the window—so, with tears of rage and pain in his eyes, he affects to be very much amused, and sorts out a bit of fish from his plate and hands it down. The cat gingerly receives it, with a look in his eyes that says: "Another time, my friend, you won't be so dull of comprehension," and purrs maliciously as he retires to a safe distance from the guest's boot before eating it. A cat isn't a fool—not by a long way.

When the family has finished tea, and gathers round the fire to enjoy the hours of indigestion, the cat slouches casually out of the room and disappears.

ANDREW BARTON PATERSON
The Cat

As I walked on the glacis I heard the sound of a bagpipe from the soldiers' dwellings in the rock, and was further soothed and affected by the sight of a soldier's cat walking up a cleated plank in a high loophole designed for muscatry, as serene as Wisdom herself, and with a gracefully waving motion of her tail, as if her ways were ways of pleasantness and all her paths were peace.

HENRY DAVID THOREAU

A speckled cat and a tame hare

Eat at my hearthstone

And sleep there;

And both look up to me alone

For learning and defence

As I look up to Providence.

WILLIAM BUTLER YEATS

Two things are aesthetically perfect
in the world—the clock and the cat.

EMILE AUGUSTE CHARTIER

Cats know how to
obtain food without
labor, shelter without
confinement, and love
without penalties.

W.L. GEORGE

❦

Cats are a tonic, they
are a laugh, they
are a cuddle, they are at
least pretty just about all
of the time and beautiful
some of the time.

ROGER CARAS

Everything a cat is and does physically
is to me beautiful, lovely, stimulating,
soothing, attractive and an enchantment.

PAUL GALLICO

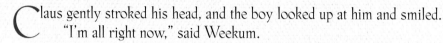

Claus gently stroked his head, and the boy looked up at him and smiled.
"I'm all right now," said Weekum.

"Yes," replied Claus, happily. "Now I will put you in my warm bed, and you must sleep until morning, when I will carry you back to your mother."

"May the cat sleep with me?" asked the boy.

"Yes, if you wish it to," answered Claus.

"It's a nice cat!" Weekum said, smiling, as Claus tucked the blankets around him; and presently the little one fell asleep with the wooden toy in his arms.

When morning came the sun claimed the Laughing Valley and flooded it with his rays; so Claus prepared to take the lost child back to its mother.

"May I keep the cat, Claus?" asked Weekum. "It's nicer than real cats. It doesn't run away, or scratch or bite. May I keep it?"

"Yes, indeed," answered Claus, pleased that the toy he had made could give pleasure to the child. So he wrapped the boy and the wooden cat in a warm cloak, perching the bundle upon his own broad shoulders, and then he tramped through the snow and the drifts of the Valley and across the plain beyond to the poor cottage where Weekum's mother lived.

"See, Mama!" cried the boy, as soon as they entered, "I've got a cat!"

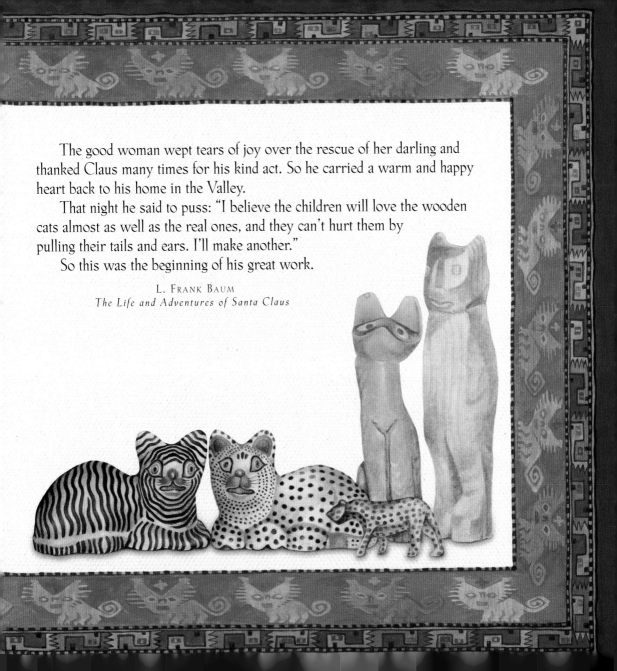

The good woman wept tears of joy over the rescue of her darling and thanked Claus many times for his kind act. So he carried a warm and happy heart back to his home in the Valley.

That night he said to puss: "I believe the children will love the wooden cats almost as well as the real ones, and they can't hurt them by pulling their tails and ears. I'll make another."

So this was the beginning of his great work.

L. FRANK BAUM
The Life and Adventures of Santa Claus

A home without a cat—
and a well-fed, well-petted
and properly revered cat—
may be a home, perhaps,
but how can it prove title?

MARK TWAIN

Most beds sleep up to six cats . . .

ten cats without the owner.

STEPHEN BAKER

For he purrs in
thankfulness, when God
tells him he's a good Cat.
For he is an instrument
for the children to learn
benevolence upon.

CHRISTOPHER SMART

With their qualities of cleanliness, discretion, affection, patience, dignity, and courage, how many of us, I ask you, would be capable of becoming cats?

FERNAND MERY

There is no domestic animal which has so radically altered its whole way of living, indeed its whole sphere of interests, that has become domestic in so true a sense as the dog: and there is no animal that, in the course of its century-old association with man, has altered so little as the cat.

KONRAD LORENZ

The cat, an animal of franker appetites, preserves his independence.

ROBERT LOUIS STEVENSON

When I play with my cat, who knows
but that she regards me more
as a plaything than I do her?

MICHEL DE MONTAIGNE

One small cat changes coming home
to an empty house to coming home.

PAM BROWN

MUPPET

GEMMA

GABRIELLE

CHESTERTON

TWIGLET

MALTEAZER